Making Live Training Lively!

50 Tips for Engaging Your Audience

Andrea Molberg, Ph.D.

A Fifty-Minute™ Series Book

This Fifty-Minute™ book is designed to be "read with a pencil." It is an excellent workbook for self-study as well as classroom learning. All material is copyright-protected and cannot be duplicated without permission from the publisher. *Therefore, be sure to order a copy for every training participant by contacting:*

1-800-442-7477 • 25 Thomson Place, Boston MA • www.courseilt.com

Making Live Training Lively!

50 Tips for Engaging Your Audience

Andrea Molberg, Ph.D.

CREDITS:
Senior Editor: **Debbie Woodbury**
Assistant Editor: **Genevieve Del Rosario**
Production Manager: **Denise Powers**
Design: **Nicole Phillips**
Production Artist: **Rich Lehl**
Cartoonist: **Ralph Mapson**

ISBN 1-56052-696-3
Library of Congress Catalog Card Number 2003115570
Printed in Canada by Webcom Limited
1 2 3 4 5 PM 06 05 04

Learning Objectives For:

MAKING LIVE TRAINING LIVELY!

The objectives for *Making Live Training Lively!* are listed below. They have been developed to guide you, the reader, to the core issues covered in this book.

THE OBJECTIVES OF THIS BOOK ARE:

❑ 1) To demonstrate how to make live training worth the investment

❑ 2) To explore ways to make learning more exciting, memorable, and fun

❑ 3) To provide proven techniques for effective seminars, classes, workshops, and conferences

❑ 4) To empower readers to be creative, dynamic trainers who make a difference

ASSESSING YOUR PROGRESS

In addition to the learning objectives above, Course Technology has developed a Crisp Series **assessment** that covers the fundamental information presented in this book. A 25-item, multiple-choice and true/false questionnaire allows the reader to evaluate his or her comprehension of the subject matter. To buy the assessment and answer key, go to www.courseilt.com and search on the book title or via the assessment format, or call 1-800-442-7477.

Assessments should not be used in any employee selection process.

About the Author

Dr. Andrea Molberg is a consulting psychologist. As a trainer, consultant, and coach, she has worked with Fortune 500 companies, governmental agencies, nonprofits, start-ups, family-owned businesses, professional associations, educational and health organizations, and individuals.

For the past 25 years Andrea has been coaching and training trainers around the country and at her regularly scheduled seminars at the Management Center of the University of St. Thomas in Minneapolis/St. Paul. A frequent conference speaker, she is also an adjunct faculty member. She teaches executive coaches at the College of Executive Coaching, MBA students at Pepperdine University's Graziadio School of Business & Management, HR professionals at UC Irvine, and executives at the Executive Education Center at UC Riverside.

Andrea holds a Ph.D. in industrial/organizational and counseling psychology from the University of Minnesota. She was selected an Outstanding Young Woman in America and chosen Teacher of the Year in Social Sciences at the University of St. Thomas, but she considers parenting two teenage daughters her greatest training accomplishment. You can reach her by e-mail at andrea@andreamolberg.com or visit her Web site at www.andreamolberg.com.

Dedication

This book is dedicated to my two daughters Alexandra Basford and Tessa Basford. They inspire me to devote the time and effort needed to make the training I conduct come alive, and they forgive me when it takes me from them. Their practical, creative ideas and frequent questions have enriched my efforts to train others up close and personal.

I am also indebted to countless students and trainers who have attended my workshops, experimented with new approaches, taken risks, generated ideas, told me their stories, and provided synergy. Thank you!

How to Use This Book

This *Fifty-Minute™ Series Book* is a unique, user-friendly product. As you read through the material, you will quickly experience the interactive nature of the book. There are numerous exercises, real-world case studies, and examples that invite your opinion, as well as checklists, tips, and concise summaries that reinforce your understanding of the concepts presented.

A Course Technology *Fifty-Minute™ Book* can be used in a variety of ways. Individual self-study is one of the most common. However, many organizations use *Fifty-Minute* books for pre-study before a classroom training session. Other organizations use the books as a part of a systemwide learning program—supported by video and other media based on the content in the books. Still others work with Course Technology to customize the material to meet their specific needs and reflect their culture. Regardless of how it is used, we hope you will join the more than 20 million satisfied learners worldwide who have completed a *Fifty-Minute Book*.

Preface

Don't worry that we trainers will become dinosaurs. Why haven't newer training approaches, such as videotapes, e-learning, or distance learning replaced seminars, workshops and breakout sessions?

There was only one year, 1993, in which organizations used another training delivery method more than they used instructor-led sessions, according to *Training* magazine's annual survey of the training industry.

The most widely used approach in that exceptional year—videotapes—did not make trainers obsolete, even though the purchase of a video for groups of trainees is a less expensive alternative. New technologies—such as e-learning, which delivers information just in time and appears more "21st century," and distance learning, which simultaneously transmits a message from a national guru to hundreds of learners in various locations—have not taken over the trainer's role either.

Organizations still schedule live training because it is worth it.

Don't get me wrong. We humans learn from a wide variety of approaches. We can acquire knowledge and skills from watching taped demonstrations or live representatives. But the experiences are not identical. Many methods of delivering training achieve results and warrant use. We develop ideas from reading, from listening to others (live or on screen), and from discussing our thoughts with others. We become more skillful from watching others perform a task and from practicing ourselves.

The point is, there are many learning options. But live training is special. Construction workers, counselors, firefighters, filmmakers, surgeons, soldiers, service representatives, salespeople, musicians, managers, pastors, and parents all receive live training—not just training by computer or video monitor. We live trainers make a difference.

This book contains training techniques proven to help others learn, techniques to help you make a difference when you create a learning environment. Enjoy sifting through this tool kit and "sharpening your saw," as Stephen Covey, author of *Seven Habits of Highly Effective People*, puts it. The more skilled, dynamic, and memorable you are as a trainer, the greater the impact you will have on the lives of those you train and then on the lives of those they serve.

Audrea Molberg, Ph.D.

Contents

Part 1: Start Off on the Right Foot

Part 2: Rev Up Participants with Your Delivery Style

Part 3: Promote Interactive Learning

Part 4: Facilitate Achievement Through Your Leadership

Part 5: Demonstrate Respect for Participants

Appendix

Why Live Training Is Worth It

What makes live training worth the cost? Interaction. Human touch. Inspiration. Motivation. Synergy. Connection. Being there is different from watching it on a screen or reading about it in a book. Organizations want training to stick, and in-person encounters are memorable.

Simply being in a learning situation with others affects our mood and attention level, which in turn affects what we remember and how committed we are later to implementing that learning. Trainers and coaches help us believe that we can master new computer systems, turn angry customers around, and solve complex problems. They teach us best practices, tricks of the trade, and shortcuts. They answer questions on the spot. Live training is up close and personal. When we are tired and frustrated, colleagues inspire us to hang in there and buddies break the monotony inherent in needed repetition. Live training offers something extra.

Peter Senge, author of *The Fifth Discipline*, has called on business and industry to become "learning organizations." In this information age, training departments rarely have to convince organizational leaders that human resources are vital to success. Most agree that knowledge and skill mean productivity, profit, and, ultimately, survival in this highly competitive, global marketplace.

Through training, people acquire the information and skills they are expected to retain and use on the job. Effective training provides employees with what they "need to know," orients them to the organization's culture, and even fosters organizational relationships necessary for individuals, teams, and organizations to succeed. Well-trained employees solve problems, please customers, save money, and generate business.

Training is a $51 billion-plus endeavor. In *Training* magazine's Annual Industry Report for 2003, 19% of companies surveyed responded "always" and 72% responded "often" when asked how often they used live instructors to deliver training. The next most commonly used instructional method was Web-based self-study, which reportedly was "always" used by 5% and "often" used by 39% of those surveyed.

Although classroom instruction is only one of many training venues, it makes sense (and cents) to invest in live training. For example, studying 40 companies and 896 individuals, the Franklin Covey Corporation reported a whopping 806% average return on investment per 22 people trained in Franklin Quest seminars.

Still, live training is worth the investment only if we make it come alive. And that is where this book comes in.

The Growing Need to Make Training Lively

Live training has become more challenging, and the trainer's task has become tougher. Today's trainers must spark involvement among widely diverse trainees with high expectations, so training professionals must be more skillful than ever before.

Now with four generations in the workforce, aging baby boomers and veterans are working beside Gen Xers and Nexters. Training sessions may include executives with advanced degrees plus workers for whom English is their second language. Trainees include the techno-phobic plus the techno-savvy. In addition, audiences today have been dazzled by the best of Hollywood. Trainees now attend seminars with critical eyes and skeptical ears.

Trainers must grab and hold their trainees' attention plus help them handle the learning experiences and the learning environment. The trainer's role includes motivating attendees to learn, as well as delivering content, ensuring retention, and facilitating application. Instructors have a lot to do. They need a complete tool kit, a wide array of strategies and skills.

How Do You Get Adult Trainees Involved?

No one approach will ensure the attention of every trainee or encourage participation all the time. That is why this book provides 50 proven tips—proven, that is, by experienced trainers who regularly face the challenge in classrooms, seminars, and conferences. You probably use many of these tools already and will recognize old favorites. You should find some new ones too. Which of these 50 tips could you dust off or add to your toolbox?

Start Off on the

Right Foot

2

Tip 1: Draw the Right People to Your Training

The best trainer in the world cannot fully compensate for a poor fit between the material and the attendees. Those in the classroom or workshop who find the training material elementary, as well as those who are lost, participate minimally at best. Successful trainers know that a disconnect between the material and the group can set a negative tone and even trigger participants to battle with the instructor.

What helps ensure that the right people attend your seminar or workshop?

➤ Avoid mandating attendance when possible. People are more likely to embrace new approaches and learn new ideas when it is their choice, not forced.

➤ Invite people who are eager to learn.

➤ Clearly publicize in advance the session objectives and any prerequisites.

Tip 2: Arrange for an Endorsement

People are more likely to be enthusiastically involved in training when their managers, informal leaders, and colleagues endorse rather than avoid the program. Which of the following approaches could you use to obtain such endorsements?

➤ Have executives recommend the seminar to those they mentor.

➤ Ask someone the participants respect to kick off the session or to send out the seminar announcement.

➤ Publish positive feedback about previous sessions or the trainer to stimulate interest.

GETTING THE WORD OUT

1. What should participants know before they come for training?

   Include some or all of the following information when announcing or publicizing training:

   ❑ Objectives

   ❑ Prerequisites

   ❑ Location

   ❑ Time

   ❑ Suggested attire

   ❑ Agenda

   ❑ Expectations and norms

   ❑ Background material

   ❑ Trainer's biographical sketch

2. How and where can you publicize your training?

   _____

   _____

   _____

   _____

   _____

3. Who could kick off your training session?

   _____

   What do you want this sponsor to say?

   _____

   _____

   _____

   _____

6

Tip 3: Tailor Your Training to the Attendees

Just as you should strive to draw the right people to your training, you also should customize the content to those who will be attending. The following are effective ways of tailoring your training accordingly.

➤ Get information about the group in advance and tailor your session to them. Use the "Know Your Participants" questionnaire on the next page to guide you in collecting this information.

➤ Through a prior needs assessment (testing, interviews, questionnaires, or observation), determine the content level that fits the attendees.

➤ Bring case studies, analogies, and examples relevant to the participants who will be attending.

➤ Obtain advance buy-in by having a focus group of participants help design the session.

➤ Invite participants to bring specific questions and cases to the session.

KNOW YOUR PARTICIPANTS

Think about a training program you are currently preparing or will be preparing soon. Answer the following questions about the participants you expect to attend. The questions in parentheses elaborate on the central question being asked. Use your answers to tailor your material to the group you will be training.

1. What do the participants *expect to gain* from the session or course? (Attendees will be wondering "What's in it for me?")

   _____

   _____

   _____

2. What is their *current level of knowledge and skills*? (How much background information or review is necessary? Will both experts and novices be attending? If so, what can you include for each? What terms will you need to clarify? What jargon would be confusing?)

   _____

   _____

   _____

3. What is their *general mood*? (Will you need to wake them up, calm them down, reduce their fears?)

   _____

   _____

   _____

4. What is their *attitude toward the topic*? (Do they dread discussing this subject? Do they think they already know it? Do they expect to be bored or confused?)

   _____

   _____

   _____

CONTINUED

5. What will they consider the *most important issues and concerns*? (What needs emphasis?)

_____

_____

_____

6. Which topics will trigger *resistance*? (Where will they disagree? What will prevent or reduce resistance?)

_____

_____

_____

7. What is their *attitude toward you*? (Are you a stranger? What is your reputation?)

_____

_____

_____

8. What is the *group size*? (Is the group so small that participants will feel pressured or so large that they might get lost in the crowd? Will they be able to see and hear? Will they have access to necessary equipment, tools, and supplies?)

_____

_____

_____

9. What are the group's *customs, norms, or rules*? (Are they used to jumping into a discussion or being lectured to? Will they expect a bathroom break on the hour?)

_____

_____

_____

CONTINUED

10. What *ages* are the participants? (Will you need to overcome generational gaps within the group or between you and them? Will the examples or training methods you use be appealing across generations?)

_____

_____

_____

11. Will the group be primarily *male, female*, or a *mixed audience*? (Will you need to use "female speak" or "male speak" communication patterns? Will your dress, language, style, and examples be appropriate?)

_____

_____

_____

12. What are the attendees' *occupations* and *job titles*? (How will they want you to refer to them? What experiences will they bring?)

_____

_____

_____

13. *Where* do attendees work (job location)? (Do they work under different conditions? Have regional concerns?)

_____

_____

_____

14. How *long* have they held their positions (job tenure)? (Are they new to the organization but not the industry?)

_____

_____

_____

15. What is their *salary range* and *socioeconomic status*? (Would certain examples or stories be inappropriate?)

_____

_____

_____

16. Do those attending have the *authority* to act on and use what they learn in training? (Will attendees have to convince their managers? If so, how can you equip them? Should you obtain management support ahead of time?)

_____

_____

_____

17. Where are attendees *from* (regional and cultural background)? (What cultural differences will you need to bridge?)

_____

_____

_____

18. Is English their *first language*? (What idioms will be unfamiliar? For example, "Let's can that idea" might be misinterpreted as "Let's preserve that," and a yardstick might be an unfamiliar measuring tool. Does the training material need translation?)

_____

_____

_____

CONTINUED

19. What is the general *educational level* of the group? (How much do participants read? What ideas have they been exposed to? Are they familiar with differing perspectives?)

_____

_____

_____

20. What are their *learning preferences* and *styles*? (Does the group consist of visual, auditory, or kinesthetic learners? Do participants prefer close contact with peers or with the trainer? Do they prefer structured vs. flowing learning environments?)

_____

_____

_____

21. Which *training methods* will appeal to the participants? (Will they prefer discussions, case studies, videotapes, demonstrations, games, hands-on situations?)

_____

_____

_____

22. Will there be participants with *special needs*? (Will there be attendees who are hearing impaired, in wheelchairs, needing an interpreter or Braille materials?)

_____

_____

_____

=CONTINUED=

12

23. How many of those attending will *know each other*? (How much will you need to break the ice? Develop trust?)

_____

_____

_____

24. What will participants *chat about* (relevant current events)? (What "hot topics" can you refer to? What is of common concern or common interest?)

_____

_____

_____

Tip 4: Take Notice of the Group Mix

The mix of the attendees in your training might signal potential challenges to optimum participation. Take note of the following and consider altering the mix of the group or seating arrangements if necessary.

➤ When attendees might be reluctant to participate in front of their managers, co-workers, or direct reports, register them in separate sessions or seat them away from each other when they come to the classroom.

➤ Avoid having only one or two representatives from a department attend a session (or sit at a table) otherwise filled entirely with participants who are already part of a different, cohesive team.

➤ Facilitate networking and cross-organizational connections, as some organizations do, by carefully planning membership and seating arrangements in training sessions.

➤ Consider having a balanced group of participants—different ages, opposite genders, mixed ethnicities, and new and long-term employees. A heterogeneous group may be slower to warm up and feel at ease with each other, but a mix of participants can offer a wide, stimulating array of ideas and perspectives.

➤ If you have a mix of generations, genders, races, and religions, include something appealing and appropriate for everyone.

Tip 5: Understand Generational Differences

In his 1998 book *Growing Up Digital*, Don Tapscott describes how learning has changed for those in the Internet generation. Learning is customized instead of one-size-fits-all, so instead of school as torture, learning becomes fun and lifelong. Hypermedia has replaced linear, sequential instruction, and teachers are now facilitators, not just transmitters. Today's learners are involved in discovering and constructing their learning rather than merely absorbing material.

Not all trainees, however, will come with these experiences, needs, and attitudes. Here is a quick overview of common generational differences:

Veterans

➤ Prefer stable, orderly, risk-free environments

➤ Are conservative conformers who respect authority

➤ Like learning tied to the organization's or society's "overall good"

➤ Value precedents and what is "tried and true"

➤ Dislike overly informal styles

➤ Want a logical summary

Baby Boomers

➤ Prefer non-authoritarian situations

➤ Are dedicated learners who expect to interact

➤ Value teamwork

➤ Respond to challenges if they see benefits

➤ Dislike role-play

➤ Want the overview

Gen Xers

➤ Prefer learning situations with lots of elbow room

➤ Are self-directed learners

➤ Expect the trainer to demonstrate expertise

➤ Ask lots of questions

➤ Like games, varied formats, role-play

➤ Want headlines, quotes, graphics, lists

Nexters (Millennials)

➤ Prefer creative learning environments with some structure

➤ Are can-do learners with a teamwork ethic

➤ Expect the trainer to encourage and help

➤ Value reducing stress and increasing marketability

➤ Are technologically savvy

➤ Want multiple focal points plus text

For more information, read "Generation Gaps in the Classroom," by Ron Zemke, Claire Raines, and Bob Filipczak, Training, November 1999.

BE PREPARED FOR DIFFERENT LEARNERS

One of the key benefits of live training is that it can be individualized for those who attend that particular session on that particular day. Without advance planning, though, trainers cannot be prepared to adjust to the current participants and will not have materials or examples ready. Effective trainers have different versions of the same case, story, and handout for different trainees.

What alterations can you make in your training content and delivery methods to achieve a better fit? Take a learning point from one of your training sessions and plan different examples, activities, and supporting material sized for different learners. One size does not fit all.

Learning Point:_____

For beginners:_____

For intermediate learners:_____

For advanced learners:_____

For auditory learners:_____

For visual learners:_____

For kinesthetic learners:_____

For introverts:_____

For extraverts:_____

For those who need structure:_____

For those who need "flow":_____

For men:_____

For women:_____

For veterans:_____

For boomers:_____

For gen Xers:_____

For millennials:_____

Compare your answers to the author's suggested responses in the Appendix.

Tip 6: Create a Welcoming Environment

Having finished your preparations for a tailor-made training program, you are ready to welcome participants and arouse their interest in getting started.

First impressions and attitudes are important. It takes more time (minutes, hours, days, weeks) and more information (data, words, reports) to change an impression than to develop one. If participants initially have a negative attitude about the facility, trainer, or session, then trainers and facilitators face an especially daunting task.

Here are proven ways to make it easy for those attending live training to immediately feel glad they came.

- Make the training room easy to find. Provide a map or detailed instructions about session location, parking arrangements, time, and attire (such as business casual), so participants arrive ready and relaxed instead of resistant or anxious.
- Arrive early and post clear, colorful, professional (but not sterile) signs outside the training room and even along the way, if the entrance is hard to find.
- Be sure that the facilities are open and comfortably bright.
- Put out the welcome mat. Inside the room, have *Welcome* printed on a flip chart or posted on a wall.
- Delight attendees' ears and set the mood with appropriate music playing in the background. (The exercise on the next page will help you brainstorm appropriate music for your participants.)
- Greet participants as they enter, just as retailers, five-star hotels, and thriving churches do. Smile warmly as you introduce yourself to participants and them to one another.
- Have only the necessary number of chairs in the room so participants feel lucky to have one. Empty tables and chairs prompt attendees to speculate about "no-shows." (Of course, have extra chairs readily available.)

➤ Help participants see their name connected to the session by having them sign in, pick up their name tag, or find their table tent card.

➤ Give attendees something right away, such as:

- Food and beverages (Note: Provide a range of beverage options. Coffee and tea may not be the beverages of choice, even in the morning, for many participants.)

- A roster of participants

- An agenda

- A lunch ticket or a list of neighboring restaurants

- Directions to restrooms and phones

- Background information on the training topic

- Publicity about upcoming training events

IN THE MOOD WITH MUSIC

Determine what musical selections you would use to create the right mood for your particular group of trainees. What would tickle their ears and set the right tone when they enter the training room? What music could be playing during breaks or as a signal to begin or end a task?

Lively and Energetic

For Traditional/Veterans:

For Boomers:

For Gen Xers:

For Nexter/Millennials:

Calming

For Traditional/Veterans:

For Boomers:

For Gen Xers:

For Nexter/Millennials:

Action Oriented (To get learners motivated for action)

For Traditional/Veterans:

For Boomers:

For Gen Xers:

For Nexter/Millennials:

Tip 7: Pique Interest in the Topic

Do not give attendees the opportunity to stare into empty space and get bored before you even begin your training. Instead, apply these tips to make people eager to start learning.

➤ Orient attendees quickly to the topic by having course objectives posted in the room, projected on a screen, or printed on a list already on the tables.

➤ Deck the training site with motivational posters or project one on a screen.

➤ Prepare attendees to get involved early by having a heading (such as *Expectations*) already printed on a flip chart page.

➤ Let participants test their current knowledge and skill with a non-threatening puzzle or quiz (think Disney's Epcot Center) or surround them with company photos or samples of your products to peruse while they wait for others to arrive.

➤ Delay distributing handout material and copies of your visuals until after the session begins. You don't want participants to read ahead and be bored later.

LIGHTS! SIGNS! ACTION!

What will you do to create a welcoming environment for your next training session?

Signs _____

_____

Lighting _____

_____

Music _____

_____

Participant's name visible _____

_____

Greeting _____

_____

Pre-session activity or materials _____

_____

Tip 8: Begin with a Bang

Making live training come alive involves grabbing people's attention and sparking their curiosity right from the start. Emulate those who know the importance of beginning with "Guess what!"

Memorize your first few sentences so you can put yourself on automatic pilot. Uptight trainers breed uptight trainees, and one of the first things to go when you are stressed is your memory and your sense of humor. Warm up, breathe deeply, and stretch, so you are relaxed and ready to begin with a bang. Otherwise, you are likely to start with something ordinary, such as, "I'm here today to teach you about..."

The following are proven grabbers for opening a stimulating session:

➤ Show a funny, topic-relevant cartoon, picture, or video clip that can be grasped visually in a few seconds. This is easier and safer than telling a joke, which hinges on good comic timing. Remember, even professional comedians have bad nights. Pretest your opener, because what is humorous to one participant is potentially insulting to another.

➤ Begin with a startling fact, graphic, or touching story.

➤ Quote someone well respected and well known.

➤ Review events leading to the need for training.

➤ Challenge participants to learn something new.

➤ Involve the participants with you in some way, such as answering a question.

➤ Convey your enthusiasm for the topic.

➤ Be passionate about participants learning from you.

PLAN YOUR GRABBER

Use the following checklist to brainstorm all the ways you could begin your training session with a bang. For each one, make a brief notation about how you could use that technique in your introduction. Use the blank lines at the end to list additional grabbers you could use.

- ❑ Present a cartoon
- ❑ Show a picture
- ❑ Run a video clip
- ❑ Tell a touching story
- ❑ Reveal a startling fact
- ❑ Display a graph
- ❑ Play an audio clip
- ❑ Tell a joke
- ❑ Share a quote
- ❑ Give a demonstration
- ❑ Explain the benefits
- ❑ Describe how the learning can be applied
- ❑ Name the consequences of not being knowledgeable or skilled
- ❑ Recap events leading to the need for training
- ❑ Detail expected results or outcomes
- ❑ Ask about the group's expectations
- ❑ Make a promise
- ❑ Propose a challenge
- ❑ Express your enthusiasm
- ❑ _____
- ❑ _____

Tip 9: Focus on Results from the Start

Right from the start, reassure training participants by your words and actions that their time will be well spent. Within the first few minutes show them that they will receive important information that will be delivered effectively. Try these strategies:

➤ Teach something practical and new immediately, so participants are eager for more.

➤ Help participants see the benefits of learning the material being delivered. They are wondering, "What's in it for me?" and "Why should I learn this?" Examples of benefits are listed on the following page.

➤ Show or explain to participants how they can apply what they learn.

➤ Point to the consequences of not being knowledgeable and skilled.

➤ Describe the payoffs, such as enhanced performance, reduced stress, and money saved; or lead participants to discover them. Both approaches work.

➤ State desired results clearly, such as, "After this session, you will be able to..."

➤ Ask the group, "What do you want to be sure we have covered by the end of this session?" or "What parts of the agenda deserve the most attention?"

➤ List the group's expectations and link the agenda to these concerns.

Promise participants they will leave knowing three new tips or having two crucial skills—and then be sure you deliver.

WHAT'S IN IT FOR ME?

Even though we do not all want the same things, the benefits of training and the learning that results can be grouped into a few major categories. Benefits come from getting something wanted (such as success) and from reducing something unwanted (such as failure).

Training helps learners...

Become	Get	Reduce	Save
able	attention	accidents	effort
accomplished	authority	anger	energy
aware	autonomy	anxiety	face
capable	better decisions	complaints	money
creative	better relationships	conflict	time
comfortable	commissions	confusion	work
competent	confidence	cost	
competitive	improved communication	discomfort	
confident	influence	distrust	
effective	job security	embarrassment	
efficient	money	errors	
influential	opportunities	frustration	
informed	options	hassles	
knowledgeable	perks	health problems	
marketable	praise	lawsuits	
motivated	prestige	pressure	
perceptive	projects	problems	
productive	promotions	rework	
profitable	raises	risk	
safe	recognition	stress	
satisfied	respect	supervision time	
secure	sales	tension	
self-confident	satisfied customers	waste	
skilled	self-esteem	worry	
successful	self-worth		
up-to-date	sense of accomplishment		
	teamwork		
	understanding		

IDENTIFY THE BENEFITS OF YOUR TRAINING

Take a moment to list how learners will benefit from a specific training situation.

Become	Get	Reduce	Save

As you develop your training program, plan ways to help learners see these benefits that you have listed.

Will you tell participants about the positive outcomes (become, gain) or negative consequences (reduce, save)?

What questions could you ask to lead participants to identify the payoffs themselves?

_____

_____

_____

Tip 10: Establish Your Credibility as a Trainer

Instructors and facilitators not only have to *be* credible, they also have to be *perceived* that way. If necessary, they can fall back on position power (the power inherent in the trainer position) for their credibility, but once you use that clout, influencing others through compatibility (being likable) becomes more difficult. A better way to establish your credibility as a trainer is to minimize your clout and rely instead on competence (having knowledge and skill), compatibility, and caring.

Adults learn from people they respect and like. We respect others for their position of authority, their expertise, and their character. Apply the following techniques to demonstrate your composure and competence.

➤ Enhance your credibility, if it is low, by having someone respected by the group introduce you or mention your association with worthwhile people and organizations.

➤ Let attendees know something of your background to show your experience and expertise.

➤ Know your material well, so you can confidently move away from your notes and the lectern.

➤ Act professional and prepared without being overly stiff or formal.

➤ Put the group at ease by dressing comfortably, appearing relaxed, and being conversational.

➤ Reduce intimidation, if your credibility is extremely high, by poking fun at yourself and showing your humanness or by making a small mistake.

➤ Be fun or funny, but not silly.

What will you do to establish your competence?

_____

_____

_____

Tip 11: Connect with Your Participants

As adults, we like those with whom we feel comfortable, and we feel comfortable with people who like us and are similar to us. That is why trainers must connect with participants. When live instructors distance themselves from the group, trainees keep their distance too. But when participants feel a connection with their trainer, they are more likely to get involved, take risks, and get the maximum benefit from the training.

➤ Connect by periodically making eye contact with each individual and holding it for a few seconds.

➤ Learn participants' names and use them.

➤ Encourage participants to call you by your first name.

➤ Establish common ground by disclosing a little personal information about yourself to show what you and the participants have in common. For example, making a reference to family usually provides a connection.

➤ Join the group by referring to something in the group's history or using some of the group's jargon.

➤ Minimize status differences by occasionally sitting down.

What do you want participants to know about you?

_____

_____

_____

Are You a Likable Trainer?

Social psychologists investigate who is attracted to whom and why. And the research on interpersonal attraction has found all of the statements listed below to be true.

➤ People like people who have the good sense to like them.

➤ People tend to form relationships with those in close proximity.

➤ Proximity leads to shared experiences.

➤ Shared experiences lead to trust.

➤ People like people and places that are familiar.

➤ People gravitate toward others with similar interests.

➤ People like people who share their beliefs and values.

➤ Being around people who are helpful and competent is rewarding.

➤ People strongly dislike those who are phonies and liars.

➤ People trust those they predict care about them.

These relationship principles can be summarized as reciprocal liking, similarity, familiarity, proximity, competence, and trust. How might you apply each one to help you relate to your trainees? Write your responses in the spaces below.

Reciprocal liking

_____

_____

CONTINUED

Making Live Training Lively!

29

Similarity

_____

_____

Familiarity

_____

_____

Proximity

_____

_____

Competence

_____

_____

Trust

_____

_____

Compare your answers to the author's suggested responses in the Appendix.

Tip 12: Show That You Care

As adult learners, we like those we trust, and we trust those whom we think care about us. So, when leading training, demonstrate early that you care that participants learn and that you believe they will learn—from you.

➤ Focus more on the group than on yourself. Ask participants about their backgrounds, preferences, concerns, and opinions. Be interested in their reactions and views. Survey the group with, "How many of you have...?"

➤ Be warm, genuine, and enthusiastic. Show you want to be there.

➤ Give the group a genuine compliment.

➤ Avoid a monotone, a "teacher" voice, or a condescending tone. Sound knowledgeable *and* collaborative.

➤ Smile often.

➤ Create a climate of trust by being predictable and consistent without being boring.

➤ Look and act like a concerned, supportive coach. Consider wearing a sweatshirt bearing a slogan, such as, "Success starts here" or "Every question is a good question."

Opening Messages

Which slogan would fit on your trainer's T-shirt or be posted on your classroom wall?

"I want you to be successful."

"Glad you're here."

"We're in this together."

"Support Team"

"Fellow Learners Welcome!"

Rev Up Participants with Your Delivery Style

Tip 13: Warm Up the Group for Participation

After giving participants a little time to get used to you and the training facilities, quickly involve them in an easy, relevant task. Icebreakers are not simply introductions; they are any activities that get attendees comfortable and participating. Active participation increases motivation, learning, and retention. To get learner involvement, you have to warm up the group. Try the following techniques.

➤ When asking attendees to speak out in front of the group, find two who seem outgoing and cooperative, then start your icebreaking activity with one of them and end with the other. Begin and end on a good note.

➤ Keep the pace fast and the activity fun.

➤ Join in. If you participate in the icebreaker, the group is likely to follow your example, especially if you prevent failure, maintain momentum, and reward involvement.

➤ To ensure that everyone understands what to do, repeat and even write initial instructions.

➤ Avoid activities (such as drawing) and topics (such as sex) that could be embarrassing, threatening, or culturally or politically inappropriate.

➤ If a participant resists, allow the person to pass, promise to come back to that person, and quickly find a willing participant. Check back with the reluctant participant another time, but be ready to move on.

➤ Create the expectation of involvement. If you sound as if you expect a fight, you will usually get one. So act as if everyone naturally will want to participate with you, and they probably will.

Tip 14: Choose Good Icebreakers

To warm up the group, initial activities should be relevant, easy, and pleasant. Useful icebreakers start participants interacting with you and each other. Choose icebreakers that facilitate networking and are compelling enough to break attendees' preoccupation with traffic, parking, unanswered phone calls, and unfinished projects. Thaw the ice by getting safe, successful participation right from the start. The following are examples of effective icebreakers.

➤ Ask participants to tell something about themselves that is "news" to everyone in the room. Assure participants that the tidbit need not be exciting or important, and explain that your purpose is simply to keep people awake and interested during introductions. Prime the pump by saying, "You might tell us something like how many cousins you have, your shoe size, your mother's middle name, what you ate for supper last night, your brush with fame, an award you won, or a pet you had." (Typically these simple facts lead to networking and are amusing and non-threatening.)

➤ Have participants list on their name tent an adjective describing themselves that starts with the first letter of their name. Then you can refer to them as "Active Andrea" or "Bashful Bob."

➤ With a group that is already acquainted, ask participants to write something about themselves that is not well known to others. Place the written facts in a jar or hat. As you draw from the hat, have the group guess the author of that fact. If possible, ask that the obscure fact relate to the training subject.

➤ Give a short true/false "pretest" about the training topic to groups of four participants to complete. Discuss the answers with the larger group as a whole.

➤ If the training topic is "Motivating Others," ask participants to discuss with a partner the characteristics of the people who have been the most influential in motivating them (such as parents, teachers, coaches, managers, mentors) or ask them to describe how those parents, teachers, and managers motivated them.

➤ In a training session on team building, provide small groups of participants with markers and flip chart paper or blank transparencies to list characteristics of the best and worst teams they have ever been a part of. Ask a representative from each small group to show and report the group's answers.

➤ Ask those attending a workshop on stress to tell you about common symptoms of stress. Record their answers on a whiteboard.

➤ Ask teams of participants in a customer service seminar to discuss what irritates customers, and record their answers on the team's posted sheet of flip chart paper. Direct the teams to go read the answers of each of the other participant teams.

➤ Invite those learning an upgraded version of software to describe frustrations they experienced with the previous version.

➤ In a workshop on meetings, list answers to the question, "What often goes wrong in meetings?"

➤ Show a picture of the work environment and have participants identify examples of safety problems.

CHECK YOUR ICEBREAKING TOOLS

Are you warming up the group with activities that meet these criteria?

➤ Topic relevant

➤ Safe

➤ Compelling

➤ Fun

➤ Easy

➤ Interactive

In the first row of the middle and right-hand columns in the following table, list two icebreakers you have used or will use. Then in the spaces provided under each activity, write the ways that each meets the criteria for a good icebreaker.

Icebreaker		
Topic relevant		
Safe		
Compelling		
Fun		
Easy		
Interactive		

Tip 15: Enliven Your Delivery

What is stimulating to one person may be irrelevant to another, so trainers must expect to "lose" everyone at some time during the training. Participants will be distracted by personal issues, unreturned phone calls, and unfinished tasks. Plus, learners can process speech at the speed of 400 to 600 words per minute, while trainers typically lecture at 125 words per minute and speak 250 words per minute in conversational bursts. People do tune out. Be prepared and prevent participants from staying tuned out for long by applying the following techniques.

➤ Elaborate and give examples related to what participants are seeing on transparencies, PowerPoint screens, and slides, rather than just reading them aloud.

➤ Illustrate with interesting analogies and memorable stories.

➤ Bring a 3-D model rather than a two-dimensional picture, or give participants pieces and let them construct the model.

➤ Capture attention by teaching one concept from one corner of the room and another from a different spot.

➤ Create games, contests, and word puzzles to reinforce terms and concepts.

➤ Discuss future applications and possible obstacles with participants, so they are thinking about the present and the future.

➤ Think about what a kindergarten teacher would do to make the subject more appealing (since everything you needed to know you learned in kindergarten!).

➤ Infuse the session with your own energy. Pick up the pace and periodically use "grabbers," as outlined on page 22, to spark interest in the next learning activity.

Tip 16: Include an Element of Surprise

For survival, people are wired to notice change. Include an element of surprise in your training so attendees can delight in the unexpected. The following are some proven techniques.

➤ Burst into song. For example, when training on the topic of change, sing the line, "And the times they are a-changing."

➤ Keep a visual aid or prop hidden until you use it. Pull something out of a bag or have something up your sleeve (literally).

➤ When discussing how the knowledge or skills will solve problems, crumple a piece of paper listing those problems or have the participants generate the list and do the crumpling.

➤ Perfect a magic trick that you can tie to course content. For example, you might make a scarf disappear as you talk about making difficult problems disappear.

➤ Add color, graphics, animation, and sound—but only *occasionally*—for effect. Startle and surprise.

➤ Let participants draw their assignment from a deck of cards.

➤ Start an important point with a drum roll.

Tip 17: Inject Some Theatrics

Your training session need not be all serious, all the time. Lighten things up and have some fun while you present your material. Here are some suggestions to spark your creativity.

➤ Bring Tom Cruise, Cary Grant, Jennifer Lopez, or Elizabeth Taylor into your session by using a celebrity name as a character in your case study or as the name on a form you are teaching others to complete.

➤ Give human characteristics to something inanimate. For example, refer to a piece of equipment the trainees use as "Betsy" or "George."

➤ Make silly comparisons, such as drawing analogies to household objects, and even bring in those props.

➤ Refer to a movie or TV series. For example, introduce a group project as "Your mission, if you are willing to accept it" or ask participants not to "vote anyone off the island." Of course, remember that learners of different ages, cultures, and genders may have different movie- and television-watching tastes. Be sure they will understand the reference.

➤ Use costumes. For example, put on different hats as you talk about managers having to fill several organizational roles or provide a customer hat and a customer service hat when you start a simulation.

Tip 18: Appeal to the Senses

Have something in the training session for people with different learning styles—auditory, visual, and kinesthetic. Auditory learners tune in to sounds, visual learners gain understanding by observation, and kinesthetics learn by doing. Keeping these styles in mind will help you understand the value of incorporating these suggestions for appealing to the senses.

➤ Bring in props, samples, short videos, or audio clips to amplify learning points. For example, play the theme song from *Jeopardy* as you quiz learners.

➤ Change media. Use overhead projectors, whiteboards, flip charts, videotapes, audiotapes, slides, and PowerPoint screens.

➤ Avoid the monotony of showing one slide after another and refrain from dulling the senses by "flying in" every bullet in PowerPoint.

➤ Provide small groups with blank transparencies or flip chart paper, so they can list their ideas and present them in visual form.

➤ To emphasize part of a handout, add color with highlighters and markers, or draw attention to content by printing certain handouts on colored paper.

➤ Decorate your learning materials with cartoon-like characters, symbols, and pictures.

Tip 19: Vary the Format and Use of Your Handouts

Handouts can be formatted in various ways to guide note taking, augment classroom discussions, and test knowledge. And the same handout sometimes can be used in several ways.

For example, the same fill-in-the-blank handout can serve as a pretest, a guided note-taking tool, and a test for understanding, depending on whether participants complete it before, during, or after a lecture. The answers to be filled in could be generated by individuals working alone; in pairs, trios, or small groups; or in one large group.

Fill-in-the-blank worksheets and course outlines are probably the most commonly used types of handouts, but there are many other formats to use, such as the following:

- Lists

- Diagrams

- Charts

- Tables

- True-false quizzes

- Matching quizzes

- Multiple-choice quizzes

- List-building questions

- Forms

- Guided note-taking sheets

- Summaries

- Supplemental reading

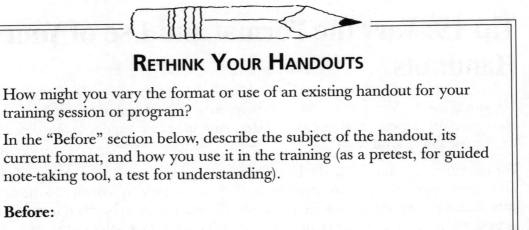

RETHINK YOUR HANDOUTS

How might you vary the format or use of an existing handout for your training session or program?

In the "Before" section below, describe the subject of the handout, its current format, and how you use it in the training (as a pretest, for guided note-taking tool, a test for understanding).

Before:

_____

_____

_____

Now rethink the handout you have just described. How might you present the same information in a different format? Review the various format options on the preceding page. How might you use the same handout in more than one way? Write your ideas in the "After" section below.

After:

_____

_____

_____

Compare your answers to the author's suggested responses in the Appendix.

Tip 20: Avoid Competing with Your Visual Aids

When you use visual aids, the group's focus is divided. But there are steps you can take, as outlined below, to keep most of the focus on you and keep distractions to a minimum.

➤ Double-check that attendees can see and hear you. Notice participant reactions and facial expressions.

➤ Face and talk to the group, not to the audiovisual equipment.

➤ To avoid blocking your visuals, stand next to them. Stand back by the screen instead of the projector. Write from the side of the flip chart. When you position yourself by the screen or easel, learners can look, listen, and remain involved without dividing their attention between you and the visual.

➤ Pick up the handout you are referring to, write its number on a whiteboard, or use colored paper for different handouts, so that you and all participants are on the same page.

Tip 21: Use a Mix of Activities

The way that learning is packaged can enliven classroom training. Today's audiences are used to channel surfing, multitasking, and being stimulated by Hollywood's special effects. Accustomed to the fast pace of life today, they have trouble just sitting still and can become bored easily.

Keep learners interested by presenting useful content in many different, compelling ways. Variety is the spice of life—and of training—so use a mix of activities, such as those suggested in the following tips.

➤ Intersperse large-group and small-group activities with brief lectures and time for individual reflection and application. Mix time alone with time for interaction.

➤ Remember that extroverted and introverted attendees have different needs. Keep learners awake without wearing them out.

➤ Include extended time with the "expert" (the trainer) and extended time exchanging ideas with peers.

➤ Change the pace. Follow demanding tasks with easier ones, and keep lectures less than 20 minutes.

➤ Divide training material into digestible chunks, providing frequent breaks.

➤ Have some groups discuss one aspect of the issue (such as the advantages) and some groups discuss another aspect (such as the disadvantages), then integrate the ideas in a large group discussion. Repetition is good, but having all participants discuss the same issue in small groups and then summarize with a large group debriefing can become redundant and therefore numbing.

Tip 22: Keep Time on Your Side

Involving a mix of activities has a high return on investment, but it does take more time than straight lecturing. Keep the following points in mind as you plan other activities to include.

➤ Schedule the right amount of time for each task or activity. Give the group a chance to warm up, yet keep an activity from dragging on.

➤ Be sure to wait for answers after asking questions and when facilitating discussion. Silence and eye contact can encourage further comments.

➤ Plan enough time and watch the clock. Otherwise, it is too tempting to revert to lecturing to cover all the learning points before time runs out.

How Will You Spice Up Live Training?

Think about a training session you will be leading in the near future. On the lines provided, list ideas for elements and techniques you could incorporate to rev up your participants and hold their interest.

Enliven your delivery

_____

_____

_____

Plan some surprises

_____

_____

_____

Add sensory appeal

_____

_____

_____

Mix in different activities

_____

_____

_____

Compare your answers to the author's suggested responses in the Appendix.

Promote Interactive Learning

Tip 23: Engage Participants in the Training

One of the key advantages of real-time training is that live trainers can construct activities and pose questions that lead participants to discover ideas and practice skills. Otherwise, trainees might as well watch a videotape or listen to a broadcast.

Outstanding teachers and coaches—who instruct, direct, and guide—use many approaches. They focus on participants and get them actively involved. Why? Because it works.

➤ Structure your live training sessions so participants are actively thinking, watching, discussing, practicing, and applying.

➤ Get participants involved with you, with one another, and with the training content. Have them wrestle with new concepts and experiment with new approaches.

➤ Provide a safe training environment where participants can try on attitudes and take calculated risks.

Tip 24: Make It Easy for People to Interact

What makes live training special, and worth the investment, is the chance to interact with the trainer and fellow trainees. Adults learn by exchanging ideas, hearing different views, and exploring various perspectives.

But sometimes trainers inadvertently or purposely discourage open communication. Instead, you need to make it easy and fun for participants to participate.

Managing real-time learning environments means encouraging people to voice their opinions and talk to one another. The following are proven ways to enable interaction.

➤ Enable participants to see and hear one another as well as seeing and hearing you.

➤ Match room arrangement to group size, room size, audiovisual equipment, and training methods. For a large group a herringbone feels more interaction-friendly than traditional classroom rows. A round table invites more discussion than does a long, rectangular one.

➤ Repeat questions and remarks from the group so everyone can hear them.

➤ Inquire further if statements are unclear or ambiguous.

Tip 25: Make It Safe for People to Participate

Sometimes getting people to interact can be difficult because they don't feel safe contributing their ideas or speaking out in front of a group. As the trainer, you can apply the following techniques to help counteract such feelings.

➤ Avoid putting an individual on the spot while letting others drop out. Toss questions to the group as a whole.

➤ Help those who resist participating to understand the benefits of doing so. For example, point out that simply watching someone else play the piano would not make you a good pianist; you would have to practice.

➤ Refer to the time for practicing skills as a "simulation" or "lab," rather than "exercise" or "role play," which might trigger negative connotations and resistance.

➤ For such activity sessions, break the group into small teams because participants find it easier to practice and make mistakes in front of a few, rather than many. Smaller groups establish contact more easily, develop cohesion faster, and get involved with the material sooner.

➤ Prevent participants from dominating or stifling others. Keep the interaction positive.

➤ Thank participants for contributing and reward those who take risks. (More about rewards is provided in Part 4.)

Tip 26: Help Participants Team Up

Many of us dreaded the times in gym class when we chose sides for volleyball or got picked (or not) to be on a baseball team. Feelings of inadequacy loomed. Adult learners often experience the same discomfort when trainers ask them to form teams or small groups. Easing this partnering process gets people faster participating.

➤ Separate the instructions for partnering up from the instructions for the learning activity. Before giving directions for an activity, first instruct participants to pair off, break into trios, or form small groups, so they are ready to interact as soon as they understand the activity.

➤ To reduce anxiety and confusion, you may sometimes select partners for attendees. Other times put participants at ease by letting them choose their own training buddies.

➤ Avoid counting off because the process is too slow. To determine group membership, place colored stickers on participants' name tags or have them draw a card from a jar on the table.

➤ Have participants move to find partners who are seated in another part of the room, so they are stimulated both by moving and by interacting with new people.

➤ Allow participants to remain with or return to previous partners with whom they are productive and comfortable, so you do not have to break the ice again.

➤ Separate resistant attendees. Divide and conquer by placing them at different tables.

Tip 27: Get People Started with Structured Interaction

Depending on the group, people can be slow to start interacting with one another, particularly if the group members were not previously acquainted. At times like these, more structure, as suggested in the following tips, rather than free-form interaction, can serve to get people started.

➤ Problems already written on a flip chart page.

➤ Toss out a challenge to get learners involved. You might set a target, such as: "With the person next to you, identify five reasons managers avoid giving negative feedback."

➤ Assign attendees tasks that necessitate interaction. For example, rotate leadership roles or provide observers a critical job to fill so they are not just "extras."

➤ Post a list of workshop norms, as shown below. Either have the group create a list or post a list of your own.

Participate!

Take risks!

Ask questions!

Contribute!

Get involved!

Tip 28: Cultivate Discussion

Because interaction is the primary benefit of live training, you'll want to continually cultivate participation. As a facilitator, you can use the following techniques to get people talking and to keep the discussion flowing.

➤ Sit down to signal that you want the group to talk.

➤ Invite participants to stop you with questions and give you examples from their own experience.

➤ When people do respond, signal your interest. Nod, smile, and say, "Yes," "Good," "More," and "What else?" to prompt additional reactions.

➤ Act as if you assume participants will interact, and directly express confidence in their willingness to jump in.

➤ If your invitation, "What questions do you have?" yields nothing, prompt the group by saying, "People often ask me...," and then give a question yourself. Your example will often pave the way for others to ask their questions.

➤ Instead of exerting tight control and directing all discussion back to you, encourage participants to answer some of the questions posed by other group members. Get out of the way, yet monitor and encourage. As participants become more interested and focused, let the group take over.

Tip 29: Ask the Right Questions

Question marks are shaped like hooks. And well-phrased, well-timed questions encourage interaction and *hook* participants into lively discussions.

When adults are talkative and relaxed, the type of question makes little difference. But to invite and facilitate discussion when participants may be hesitant, open-ended questions typically yield the most interaction. Open-ended questions can be direct or indirect.

Open-ended *direct* **questions:**	**Open-ended** *indirect* **questions:**
➤ *What?* ➤ *Why?* ➤ *How?*	➤ *Tell me about ...* ➤ *Please describe...* ➤ *Help me understand...* ➤ *Give me an example of...* ➤ *That happens because...*

Using only direct questions can seem like the Spanish Inquisition to some people. In particular, the question "Why?" has been called the most accusatory interrogative. Hearing that question makes some people believe they have to have the one, perfect answer or that they must defend themselves. Less defense-arousing alternatives include "What do you think triggered that?" or "I'm wondering why..."

Incomplete questions or sentences also signal others to respond. Ask "What else..." and then let your voice trail off to imply "What else can you think of or suggest?" Or say "That means...," letting your voice trail off, leaving the sentence unfinished. If you wait and appear to expect a response, you will probably get one.

Leading or biasing questions, by contrast, suggest the desired answer and may prevent you from getting the information you need. For example, when asked, "You don't have any problems with that, do you?" most participants will refrain from mentioning any problems they have. Open-ended questions will give you a better window into their world.

Limit Discussion with Closed-Ended Questions

Sometimes facilitators must restrict discussion rather than promote it. Use closed-ended questions when your purpose is to clarify, verify, or limit discussion.

Closed-ended questions restrict answers, as in the following examples:

➤ Have you tried this before? (answer *yes* or *no*)

➤ Do you want to work on this alone or with a partner? (choose one)

Note that even when you ask closed-ended questions, talkative folks still may fail to notice your attempt to limit their answers and may offer more than the asked-for response.

CHOOSING THE RIGHT HOOK

Identify each of the numbered examples that follow by the type of question or statement it represents. Write the letter of the question type in the space before each example.

A. Open-ended direct question
B. Open-ended indirect question
C. Incomplete sentence
D. Closed-ended question
E. Leading question

___1. What do you recommend?

___2. Is this what you recommend?

___3. I'm wondering if you had a similar experience.

___4. Did you have a similar experience?

___5. An example of that would be...

___6. An example of that would be:

    a. Jack's client

    b. Chris' customer

    c. Pat's colleague

___7. Should that be done before or after you call security?

___8. When should that be done?

___9. Please tell me which terms are most confusing.

___10. You know all this, don't you?

Compare your answers to the author's suggested responses in the Appendix.

Tip 30: Apply Active Learning Techniques

Adult learners will especially remember what they *do* during a training session. So don't just tell and show, but also let learners *do*. New drivers must get behind the wheel and push the gas pedal, not just watch or listen to experienced drivers. After you explain and demonstrate, let participants practice. Activate your training with the following techniques.

➤ Have participants analyze cases, generate examples, answer questions, and complete projects alone and also with the help of other learners. Plan time for listening, watching, and doing.

➤ Challenge participants with relevant puzzles and interesting games (as on *Jeopardy* or *Who Wants to Be a Millionaire?*) that make repetition fun.

➤ Instead of simply lecturing about how to complete a form, have the participants complete the form with you.

➤ Develop icons to jog learners' memories and have them guess the relevant point connected to each icon, or give them the task of developing the icons.

➤ Place participants in positions where they can examine different perspectives. For example, have them argue on behalf of those in favor of a change and also those opposed to it, or have them take the role of both a manager and the problem employee the manager is coaching.

➤ Pause in the middle of a lengthy videotape and ask the participants to discuss relevant issues or give examples from their own experience.

Tip 31: Invite Participants to Take the Lead

Throughout your training sessions, toss the conversational ball, and when possible, ask instead of tell.

➤ Rather than outlining obvious consequences, ask participants to tell you about those consequences. Similarly, invite them to tell you common symptoms and add only the important ones they forget.

➤ Provide a list of ideas and ask participants to break into small groups and select the three best ideas so they will read and discuss the listed ideas rather than listen to you lecture.

➤ Present course content as a list of true-false questions and have teams debate the answers.

➤ Provide participant teams with a handout summarizing learning points and then ask them to deliver the material to the rest of the group. Give the teams preparation time to develop a panel discussion, skit, commercial, or press conference as their delivery mode. Or have teams craft and present a picture, "Top Ten" list, PowerPoint slide, poem, or song.

Tip 32: Have Trainees Summarize Learning Points

Trainees will have a sense of teaching themselves if you give them the task of summarizing the learning points of the training or a section of training. Try these sample techniques for active summaries.

➤ Give small groups of participants an acronym (such as "SERVICE") and ask them to list customer service attitudes and approaches they have learned that begin with each letter. For SERVICE, the result might be:

Smiling

Eager

Responsive

Visually connected

Inquiring

Caring

Energetic

➤ After a mini-lecture describing a six-step process, pass out six cards, each naming one of the six steps, to six participants. Then ask the six to stand and arrange themselves, in order, to show how the process works.

➤ Provide transparencies and markers so small groups of attendees can draw two symbols or pictures to cue their memories. Have the other groups guess what learning points the pictures represent.

➤ Ask those learning new software to shout (like a cheer) the four required fields that must be completed on a computer screen.

➤ In lieu of simply asking, "Do you have any questions?" test their understanding. Ask them, "What was the second step?" or "What has to be on a check to make it a 'negotiable instrument'?"

➤ For advanced learners, provide note cards so they can write two difficult questions testing mastery of the training material. Let them pose their questions to another group to see if they can stump them.

➤ Distribute a fill-in-the-blank, matching, or multiple-choice test to be completed in pairs or trios. Review the answers with the large group.

➤ Assign small groups of attendees the task of writing a short press release describing the seminar's main learning points.

➤ Ask participants to develop a job aid outlining the crucial steps they have learned. Laminate the aid for everyone to take back to their job.

HOW WILL YOU ENGAGE PARTICIPANTS IN TRAINING?

Plan for active involvement and select learner-centered (not instructor-focused) activities that will enable participants to learn and retain the material.

1. When will participants discuss ideas, concepts, and application?

   _____

   _____

   _____

2. When will participants be watching?

   _____

   _____

   _____

3. What will participants do?

   _____

   _____

   _____

4. What skills will participants practice?

   _____

   _____

   _____

5. When will you have participants applying what they are learning?

   _____

   _____

   _____

6. How can you test and check their understanding?

   _____

   _____

   _____

Facilitate Achievement Through Your Leadership

Tip 33: Keep Participants on the Right Track

In live training, instructors serve to increase the chances participants will succeed. They do this by guiding, explaining, inspiring, prodding, and encouraging. They put people at ease. They add or delete content and adjust delivery speed and style. They notice who is confused and then actively reduce learning barriers. Trainers make learning possible.

How can trainers help participants to relax, understand, and learn? What helps attendees to achieve in the training program and back on the job?

➤ Start with easier material to build a history of success and then move from familiar content to new training material. Link the unknown to the known for positive transfer.

➤ Provide memory cues (such as acronyms and icons) and memory joggers (such as job aids and summaries).

➤ Show the group where you are going. Preview what happens next and then follow your outline so participants are not lost.

➤ Periodically check for understanding by testing what participants are acquiring. Or have them summarize the learning points as in Tip 32.

➤ Help participants understand the big picture as well as individual learning points. Focus on the sessions' goals and objectives and remind participants what you want them to retain and apply.

➤ Explain the reasons behind procedures, because the more that adults understand why, the more likely they are to get involved, learn, and remember what is being taught. Meaningful material is memorable.

Tip 34: Give Clear Instructions

Trainers can help ensure that participants have positive experiences by providing clear, succinct instructions before any activity. Following these guidelines will help prepare participants for learning and will keep them moving forward.

➤ Use the **KISS** approach (**K**eep **I**t **S**hort and **S**imple) to teach concepts, skills, and values.

➤ Because people get distracted, repeat directions or also present them in writing so participants can review them.

➤ Divide big tasks into smaller steps, taking them one at a time in sequence and then linking them together. Slowly and patiently demonstrate each segment of a large process.

➤ Avoid confusing jargon. Define terms and acronyms as you use them so trainees can learn the lingo. Speak in language they understand.

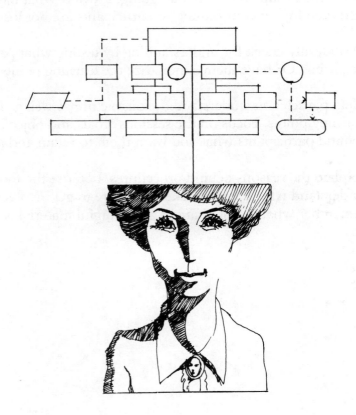

WRITE CLEAR INSTRUCTIONS

Below are some confusing instructions for a small group activity. Rewrite them on the lines provided so that the participants who are seated at tables can willingly jump in and learn.

"Now it is time to practice reaching a consensus in a meeting. You are trying to develop a list of criteria for selecting the PPC chair. You are one of five members of a selection committee. You'll only be meeting for half an hour in this fishbowl in three rounds of 10 minutes each. Since there are 25 of us in class, 20 will be observers of the fishbowl and provide consultation to the committee members. Between the rounds, those on the committee will have an opportunity to meet with the observers assigned to them for advice on both the criteria list (content) and the way the committee is reaching its decision (process). Pick one person from your table to be part of the committee sitting in the inner circle, the "fishbowl." The consultation sessions between rounds are three minutes long. The committee should agree on the five most important selection criteria in order by the end of Round 3; that is your mission. The person who has the earliest birthday is the person from your table on the committee, and the rest of you are that person's consultants or observers. After the third round, we'll discuss what you saw and experienced. This is called a fishbowl, since many of you will be watching others practice meeting and consensus-reaching skills. Observers should sit in the outer chairs directly facing the representative from their table. Everyone understands, right?"

_____

_____

_____

_____

_____

_____

_____

_____

_____

Compare your answers to the author's suggested responses in the Appendix.

Tip 35: Ensure Success

The trainer's job differs from an entertainer's or speaker's. Trainers are successful not just when the audience is informed and entertained, but when trainees learn and retain. Follow these strategies to ensure that participants keep absorbing the material.

➤ Use pilot-tested activities that can be accomplished successfully. Know how long an exercise takes and what participants need.

➤ Before turning a group loose, check their understanding by having someone summarize the directions for the assigned task.

➤ Anticipate trouble and have contingency plans. Bring another case to analyze or a second example to illustrate a difficult concept.

➤ When necessary, adjust your training design to increase success.

➤ Be sure to have all necessary equipment, pencils, handouts, and so on. If necessary, prepare for participants with special needs: Have Braille handouts, sound amplifiers, handicap-accessible training areas, and sign language interpreters.

➤ Take a break when the group is tired.

Tip 36: Maintain a Supportive Environment

When their efforts lead to success, trainees remain engaged and work to learn more. Apply these techniques to keep participants moving toward success.

➤ Protect everyone's self-esteem and set people up for success.

➤ Provide needed guidance without interfering or dominating, and intervene when participants are dominating or hindering others.

➤ Minimize excessive competition and fear of failure. Allow attendees to learn with the help and support of a partner or team.

➤ Spend time with all learners.

➤ Manage the time so participants will succeed. Prepare the group to complete their work by giving them a two-minute warning. (Hint: Use a timer or stopwatch to interrupt the learning activity so participants don't "resent" you personally when time runs out.)

➤ Quit on a winner, while participants are still engaged and having fun.

➤ Maintain a can-do spirit, because enthusiasm is contagious and positive attitudes lead to success.

What do you do to help keep learners learning? Give yourself credit as you list your methods below.

_____

_____

_____

_____

_____

Tip 37: Use Course Content to Reinforce Learning

Your goal as the trainer is not only to teach the course content to your trainees, but also to help them retain what they learn. You can facilitate this by applying the following techniques along the way to reinforce the lessons of the training.

➤ Whenever possible, seize "teachable moments" by immediately answering participants' questions.

➤ If you need to delay answering a question, write the question on a Post-it®, whiteboard, or flip chart (a "parking lot") to show that you intend to return to the question. Be sure to answer "parked" questions and then check them off when you have.

➤ Periodically remind attendees why the training material is important and "what's in it for them" by referring to the benefits you established earlier.

➤ Dramatize training benefits by charting participants' progress, showing pictures of happy customers, or quoting satisfied learners from earlier training sessions.

Tip 38: Reinforce Participant Involvement

Participants typically get involved and stay involved in classrooms and workshops if:

➤ Involvement with the instructor is pleasant

➤ Involvement with the group of fellow trainees is pleasant

➤ They consider the specific learning activity fun or relevant

➤ They are learning something they want to learn

➤ They perceive a reason to learn

➤ They receive a payoff (such as token gifts, applause, a smile, points, candy) for participating and volunteering

That basic learning principle—reinforcement—is simple. But reinforcing participation during live training sessions is not. What is rewarding to one participant (for example, public praise) is not rewarding to another. And although some may find praise rewarding in one situation, they may not in another setting.

So what is a trainer to do? Use a mix of verbal and non-verbal, internal and external reinforcement, and notice whether participants react positively. Reinforcement should feel pleasant (not silly or embarrassing) to the recipient.

What Will Your Trainees Find Rewarding?

- ❑   Interaction with the trainer
- ❑   Supportive colleagues
- ❑   Fun learning activities
- ❑   Useful content (knowledge or skills)
- ❑   Friendly competition
- ❑   Incentives, prizes, awards
- ❑   _____
- ❑   _____
- ❑   _____

The tips on the following pages will give you specific ideas on how to reinforce participant involvement during training.

Tip 39: Catch Trainees Doing Things Right

Everyone learns in Psych 101 that the way to reinforce good behavior in children is to recognize them when they do things right. The same principle holds true for adult learners. Acknowledge the actions you want them to take and you are sure to get more of the "right" responses and behaviors throughout the training. Try the acknowledgments that follow.

➤ Orally acknowledge effort or collaboration with statements such as "I noticed how you helped your group."

➤ Listen, nod, smile, and paraphrase when participants comment and contribute.

➤ Show excitement—change your voice, widen your eyes, move closer—when people demonstrate they have learned the material.

➤ Confirm right answers by providing scores (as on tests) that indicate achievement or mastery.

➤ Thank participants. Tell them you appreciate their questions, observations, and assistance.

Tip 40: Reinforce Involvement by Recording Contributions

When someone writes down our comments or takes note of what we said, we usually feel respected and valued. Recording involvement in a training session reinforces participation and motivates adult learners to continue participating. Plus, writing responses during live training gets the point both heard and seen.

How can trainers capture and display contributions? With markers or pens or computer keyboards. Quick, accurate recording is the key.

➤ To reward participation during a group discussion, be careful to list every response. If you list some, list all.

➤ Write exactly what participants say, but not necessarily all of what they say. You might paraphrase aloud, but show respect by jotting down their contributions whenever possible without changing the wording.

➤ Abbreviate and write rapidly to keep the discussion lively. (This isn't the time to be concerned about penmanship or spelling, so you can joke about not having spell check.)

Tip 41: Encourage Responses with List-Building Techniques

Confronting a blank sheet on a flip chart can be inhibiting, so apply the following techniques to stimulate involvement.

➤ Have a large, colorful heading printed on the easel to both focus discussion and fill up the space.

➤ Write big, especially at first, as shown in the example below, where the bolded items were written first. This way, psychologically at least, the list seems longer than it already is.

➤ Resist turning to a second, blank flip chart page unless you are confident that the group can fill it. Instead, jot down answers along margins to create the impression of abundance.

➤ Signal that you are expecting many responses by putting a column of bullets on a flip chart.

➤ When recording on a flip chart or whiteboard, be sure everyone can see. To show the list to larger groups, write on blank transparencies on the overhead projector or type into the computer for projection overhead.

Flip Chart Benefits

Create momentum.
Respect contributions by not placing them in a particular order.

Reward involvement.
Reduce "writer's block."

Record suggestions.
Abbrev. to capture ideas quickly.
Keep all ideas visible.

Write exactly what the participants say—in their own words

Tip 42: Avoid Pitfalls in Recording

To keep the session informal and flowing, sometimes it is better to refrain from recording. Listing contributions can slow down idea generation if:

➤ The scribe cannot keep pace

➤ Participants start paying attention to the process rather than the discussion points

➤ The discussion seems forced and stilted

Should you ask someone else to write for you? It is best to perfect your own list-building skills. Participants may get caught up in watching the scribe, or the scribe may start rewording some answers.

If important points are not surfacing from the group, add ideas to the record after the group has had time to think and after the discussion is under way. Gently and occasionally interject your ideas one at a time to avoid stifling others. Phrases such as "Oh, that reminds me..." and "May I piggyback on that?" help keep trainers from appearing too domineering.

Be sure the discussion topic is crystal clear, so you will have something to record.

Tip 43: Get Participants Writing

Recording contributions need not be limited to the trainer calling for responses from the whole group. You can stimulate trainee-to-trainee interaction by involving small groups in their own discussion and recording sessions.

➤ Have small groups of participants stand at easels, listing their own answers to discussion questions. Then direct them to move as a unit to another group's easel to see if other teams generated different responses.

➤ Provide note cards or Post-its® for participants to record their ideas, and then post their thoughts for the group to look at during breaks. Or print and distribute a master list later.

➤ Encourage friendly competition by having each small group of participants record their answers and ideas on different colored Post-its® or note cards. The colors will make it easy to spot the teams with the most answers.

What other ideas do you have to get participants writing? Record your ideas below so you can refer to them later as you prepare for your live training session.

_____

_____

_____

_____

_____

_____

_____

_____

_____

Tip 44: Build Rewards into the Training Session

People do what they get rewarded for doing. So it makes sense to stimulate involvement by providing small rewards throughout the training.

➤ Monitor group interest and energy levels. Provide frequent breaks and infuse the session with your own energy and enthusiasm—or with caffeine and sugar.

➤ Reward participants' timely returns from breaks by beginning each module with a bang, as outlined in Tip 8.

➤ Reward prompt and participating attendees by giving them choices or decisions in the training session. For example, let participants who return promptly after breaks determine who will (or will not) be the group spokesperson in the next list-building discussion.

➤ Tie the length of the break or the end of the session to the number of ideas or answers generated. For example, when participants identify 10 suggestions, they earn 10 extra minutes of break time or the chance to leave 10 minutes early.

➤ Create small contests (such as *Jeopardy*) between teams of participants and have consolation prizes too.

➤ Give participants points or candy when they volunteer or complete a learning task.

➤ After finishing a project, let participants choose a token gift from a "basket of goodies" (such as coffee mugs, pens, toys, or funny Post-it® notes).

➤ Laugh and have fun, but at no one's expense.

PLAN FOR ACHIEVEMENT

Learning seldom just "happens." As a trainer, you must guide, explain, inspire, prod, and encourage to help participants achieve the training goals. Answer the following questions in the spaces provided to explore how you might improve your training methods.

1. Think of a time when participants found a training session especially difficult. What would have helped them succeed?

   _____

   _____

   _____

2. Giving clear instructions takes planning. Write out detailed directions for a difficult section of your training.

   _____

   _____

   _____

3. Know what you want participants to achieve, discover, or produce. What will you do to help them achieve? Set goals and write them below.

   _____

   _____

   _____

4. Practice doesn't make perfect, but it does make permanent. Plan creative ways to build in repetition and facilitate retention, and write your ideas below.

   _____

   _____

   _____

Demonstrate Respect for Participants

Tip 45: Treat Participants as Colleagues

When respected, participants are more receptive, open-minded, and ready to learn.

➤ Minimize status differences and excessive formality. You will appear more comfortable and relaxed in general if you periodically sit, move, and come out from behind the lectern.

➤ Collaborate and work together with trainees. When you need assistance during a training session, ask for it with "Help me out."

➤ Freely exchange ideas and experiences. Remember that adults come to training with a wealth of experience and knowledge. Learn from them and let them learn from one another.

➤ Invite training participants to interrupt with comments, questions, and observations.

➤ Jointly set training norms or "rules."

➤ Give adults choices (where to sit, which small group to join, which issue to tackle).

➤ Throughout the session, encourage participants to share what they know and to learn from each other. Facilitate learning rather than being a know-it-all or the sole source of knowledge. Use the active learning techniques from Tip 30.

➤ Challenge participants without competing with them or getting into a power struggle. Your competence does not hinge on their incompetence, but your compatibility does hinge on being compatible.

Tip 46: Speak Respectfully

In keeping with treating participants as colleagues, trainers and facilitators should remember to teach, not preach. After all, training is basically conversation with a purpose, so it is best to be conversational and respectful as the following tips suggest.

➤ Suggest and request rather than command and demand. Use the magic words *please* and *thank you.*

➤ Ask participants for their opinions using open-ended questions instead of biasing and leading ones, which you learned about in Tip 29.

➤ Respect participants' ideas, knowledge, and experience by listening and paraphrasing.

➤ Point out when and where you agree.

➤ Choose words that suggest flexibility and openness rather than rigidity and judgment. For example, when possible, substitute *often* for *always.*

➤ Acknowledge and honor differing views by supportively responding, "Yes, that's another way to look at it."

➤ When you must correct an obviously wrong answer, say something such as, "I wish the research supported that," "I wish I could agree," or "Many people felt that way until they found ..."

➤ Practice responses to tough questions. Anticipate and answer objections before they intensify, and use the fogging technique in the tip that follows to respond to attack. Use a pleasant voice tone rather than sounding condescending or patronizing.

➤ Pay attention to your non-verbal communication to avoid unintentionally signaling disrespect. Keep your hands off your hips, a scowl off your face, and your fingers out of participants' faces.

Tip 47: Use the Fogging Technique to Mitigate Tension

When training gets tense or you need to cool down in the face of a tough participant, use the technique known as *fogging*, which means coping by agreeing calmly. This alternative to denying or retaliating is a way to act and appear calm until you actually are. Because this is acting, you need a well-rehearsed script. With the phrases memorized, you can concentrate on your style of delivering that script.

Listen to exactly what was said and find something you can honestly agree with. Then say something like:

➤ *"You're right"* or *"Yes, that's true."*

➤ *"You may be right"* or *"There could be some truth in that."*

➤ *"Oh, it could look that way."*

For example, if someone attending your session says, "You shouldn't be spending so much time on this," how could you reply?

➤ *"Hmmm, you might have a point there."*

➤ *"It certainly might appear that way."*

➤ *"That may very well be."*

Fogging involves agreeing with surface truth, possible truth, or some principle, without sarcasm. Voice tone, posture, and facial expressions are crucial. Avoid denying, defending, counterattacking, and being sarcastic.

Once the tension has eased and you are back under control, go ahead and tactfully present your differing view. Fogging is an excellent short-term answer. Using a fogging phrase buys time until you can skillfully proceed.

Tip 48: Avoid Triggering Defensiveness

When threatened or fearful, people revert to habitual ways of reacting. They get so caught up in protecting their self-esteem that they are too busy to learn, listen, understand, or collaborate. Defensive people will resist trying on unfamiliar perspectives, acquiring skills, or experimenting with new approaches. Then learning decreases because defending a viewpoint makes embracing a different one more difficult. If belittled, participants shift their focus from learning to proving their worth. That is why it is important to reduce defensiveness in the training sessions you lead.

In his classic works on defensive communication, psychologist Jack Gibb described behaviors and styles that trigger defensiveness and those that help create a supportive, non-defensive climate. The two lists that follow highlight the differences between a defensive-arousing learning climate and a more supportive one.

Defensive-Arousing	Defensive-Reducing
Judgmental	Descriptive
Controlling	Problem-Oriented
Manipulative	Genuine
Indifferent	Caring
Condescending	Respectful
Certain	Open-Minded

Is your style defensive-reducing or defensive-arousing?

Remember, avoiding defensiveness altogether is easier than reducing it. And the key to avoiding defensiveness is respecting training participants as capable adults.

Tip 49: Maintain High Expectations

One of the most effective ways for trainers and facilitators to broadcast their respect for participants during training is by setting, expressing, and maintaining high expectations for what they will be able to learn. You can communicate these expectations throughout the training session in the following ways.

➤ Set high, achievable expectations for skill mastery, or ask participants to do so.

➤ Ask participants to share the responsibility for making the training useful.

➤ To demonstrate that you expect participants to implement what they have learned, ask them during the session to discuss when and how they will apply the training later.

➤ Remind participants that on-the-job application is in their hands.

Tip 50: Celebrate Accomplishments

You're done! But don't just say good-bye and be done with it. The final moments—or the last half hour or so—are a time for final reinforcement of the course objectives. This is also the time for all to celebrate the accomplishment of their goals. Here are some ideas for doing both.

➤ Encourage participants to report what they have learned and will take away with them.

➤ Applaud, cheer, and whistle.

➤ Distribute certificates or medals signifying that participants completed the training or successfully passed a test of the training material.

➤ Play "Pomp and Circumstance" and shake participants' hands as they leave.

➤ Celebrate the end of training with a pizza party, tickets to a sporting event, movie passes, or gift certificates to a local restaurant.

➤ Make participants glad they came and got involved.

A P P E N D I X

Stay Relevant by Being Effective

In every live training situation, there are countless opportunities to make the session become even more lively. Keep exploring ways to add excitement, especially by planning for participant involvement. Help those who attend feel safe, adequate, and glad they came. Grab their attention. Structure for success and achievement. Invite and reward interaction.

These are proven training techniques. You probably use many of these tools already and recognize old favorites. Hopefully, you found some new approaches too. Which training strategies might you be dusting off or adding to your toolbox?

When participants are actively engaged with you, with one another, and with the material, they are too busy to be bored or to pick you apart. Plus, most important, they are *learning*. When participants acquire, retain, and apply, then coaches and trainers have been successful.

And as long as live training is effective, live trainers will be in demand.

GOING LIVE!

Describe a training opportunity you will be preparing for soon:

_____

_____

What will be your biggest challenges in delivering that training?	Which techniques in this book will help you succeed at those challenges?
➤ Creating a welcoming environment	
➤ Drawing the right people	
➤ Beginning with a bang	
➤ Being someone that participants want to learn from	
➤ Breaking the ice	
➤ Adding variety and spice	
➤ Using active learning techniques	
➤ Promoting interaction	
➤ Facilitating achievement	
➤ Rewarding involvement	
➤ Recording contributions	
➤ Treating participants as colleagues	

CONTINUED

➤	Celebrating accomplishments	
➤	Other:	

Author's Suggested Responses to Exercises

Be Prepared for Different Learners (Page 16)

Learning Point: Steps in the problem-solving process

For beginners: Teach 6 steps: (1) analyze problem, (2) generate solutions, (3) evaluate solutions, (4) decide, (5) implement, and (6) reassess.

For intermediate learners: Add the concepts of divergence, assimilation, convergence, and accommodation

For advanced learners: Add learning style orientations from The Kolb Learning Style Inventory published by HayGroup.

For auditory learners: Play a song (jingle) listing the steps.

For visual learners: Show a model of the steps using PowerPoint.

For kinesthetic learners: Have participants place six blocks marked *analyze problem, generate solutions, evaluate solutions, decide, implement,* and *reassess* in the correct order.

For introverts: Have participants individually complete a worksheet identifying the correct sequence.

For extraverts: Have small groups of participants complete a worksheet identifying the correct sequence.

For those who need structure: Discuss and list advantages of following this sequence before discussing disadvantages.

For those who need "flow": Simultaneously discuss advantages and disadvantages of following the sequence.

For men: Use example of choosing which truck to purchase

For women: Use example of choosing which outfit to purchase

For veterans: Use large font on handouts

For boomers: Use informal, inclusive language on handouts

For gen Xers: Add example of success for credibility

For millennials: Add more directions for problem-solving role play

Are You a Likable Trainer? (Pages 29–30)

Reciprocal liking: Tell the group "I'm glad you came."

Similarity: Mention common experiences such as "We all have been customers."

Familiarity: Refer to something that has already happened during the training session, such as "That ties in with what you just suggested, Chris."

Proximity: Sit among the participants rather than standing behind a podium.

Competence: Let the participants know "I've had success with this."

Trust: Do what you say you will do, so if the agenda says the break is at 10:00 A.M., be sure to break then.

Rethink Your Handouts (Page 44)

➤ Convert an outline into a guided note-taking handout with a lot of blank space.

➤ Turn a list of terms into a matching quiz to be completed in a small group.

➤ Transform lecture notes into a list of items for a true-false quiz to be given before as a needs assessment tool or after as a check for understanding.

How Will You Spice Up Live Training? (Page 48)

Enliven your delivery: Find a startling statistic for a seminar on burnout such as "Leisure time has dropped more than 40% in the last 20 years," and have the group discuss what that percentage or statistic is. Then reveal the answer.

Plan some surprises: When teaching how to deal with an irate customer, have someone barge into the room acting upset, so you can demonstrate how to calm someone down.

Add sensory appeal: Insert a funny, topic-relevant comic into your PowerPoint presentation.

Mix in different activities: Have teams of participants create an acronym to help them remember your main points or the steps for completing a task.

Choosing the Right Hook (Page 59)

Answers to matching quiz:

1. A (open-ended direct)	6. D (closed-ended)
2. D (closed-ended)	7. D (closed-ended)
3. B (open-ended indirect)	8. A (open-ended direct)
4. D (closed-ended)	9. B (open-ended indirect)
5. C (incomplete sentence)	10. E (leading)

Write Clear Instructions (Page 69)

You might tell your group something like this:

"Now it is time to practice reaching a consensus. Pick one person from your table who will be part of a committee and who will be attending a committee meeting. If no one volunteers, the person who has the earliest birthday (for example, January 3 instead of March 30) becomes the committee member, and the rest of you at the table are that person's consultants or observers. Once you've determined who that committee person is, I'll give you further instructions.

"Okay, would the one committee person from each table please move to a chair in the inner circle. That will be the "fishbowl." Thanks. This is called a fishbowl because the rest of you will be watching these five committee members meet and reach a consensus. Observers please sit in the outer circle chairs directly facing the person representing your table as shown in the diagram. Great.

"Fishbowl members, you are the selection committee who will be assigned to pick the chair of the 'Peak Performance Council.' That council's job is to suggest ways to help everyone in the organization become a peak performer. Your task now is to develop a list of criteria for selecting the chairperson. As a selection committee, you will meet in this fishbowl in three 10-minute rounds for a total of 30 minutes. Between rounds, you will have an opportunity to meet with your observers for 3 minutes for advice on both the criteria list (content) and the way the committee should reach agreement (process). Your mission is to agree on the five most important selection criteria, in order, by the end of Round 3.

"Observer/consultants, you should be sitting so that you can see and hear the representative from your table. Your job is to provide advice on both the content and process of the committee's meeting. After the third round, we'll all discuss as a large group what you saw and what the committee experienced as you worked to reach a decision.

"Would someone be willing to summarize the activity, so I can clear up any confusion?"

Some more suggestions:

Because the instructions are complicated, separate the directions for teaming up from the instructions for the activity. Write some of the instructions on a board or flip chart so participants can both see and hear them as well as refer back to them if necessary and even provide a picture of the seating arrangement. Having the instructions and a diagram on a handout would be another way of ensuring success.

The handout could include:

Mission:	List in order the five most important criteria for selecting the chair of the Peak Performance Council.
Fishbowl Round 1:	10 minutes
Consultation:	3 minutes
Fishbowl Round 2:	10 minutes
Consultation:	3 minutes
Fishbowl Round 3:	10 minutes
Large group discussion:	*What helped the committee reach a consensus?*
	What made reaching a consensus difficult?
	What skills were used?
	What else would have helped?

[Insert drawing of five chairs in the center of a ring of 20 chairs]

Recommended Reading

Barker, Kathryn. "Return on Training Investment: An Environmental Scan and Literature Review." *FuturEd*, June 2001.

Charney, Cy, and Kathy Conway. *The Trainer's Tool Kit*. NY: Amacom, 1998.

Eitington, Julius E. *The Winning Trainer, Third Edition*. Houston, TX: Gulf Publishing, 1996.

Hart, Lois B. *Training Methods That Work*. Menlo Park, CA: Crisp Publications, 1991.

Kearny, Lynn. *Graphics for Presenters*. Menlo Park, CA: Crisp Publications, 1996.

McArdle, Geri. *Delivering Effective Training Sessions*. Menlo Park, CA: Crisp Publications, 1993.

Pikurich, George, Peter Beckschi, and Brandon Hall. *The ASTD Handbook of Training Design and Delivery*. NY: McGraw-Hill, 2000.

Silberman, Mel. *Active Training: A Handbook of Techniques, Designs, Case Examples, and Tips*. San Diego, CA: Lexington Books, 1990.

Smith, Barry, and Brian Delahaye. *How to Be an Effective Trainer, Second Edition*. NY: John Wiley & Sons, 1987.

Tapscott, Don. *Growing Up Digital*. NY: McGraw-Hill, 1998.

Van Daele, Carrie. *50 One-Minute Tips for Trainers*. Menlo Park, CA: Crisp Publications, 1996.

Zaccarelli, Brother Herman. *Training Managers to Train, Third Edition*. Menlo Park, CA: Crisp Publications, 2004.

Making Live Training Lively!

VERM

CRISP WORLDWIDE DISTRIBUTION

English language books are distributed worldwide. Major international distributors include:

ASIA/PACIFIC

Australia/New Zealand: In Learning, PO Box 1051, Springwood QLD, Brisbane, Australia 4127   Tel: 61-7-3-841-2286, Facsimile: 61-7-3-841-1580
ATTN: Messrs. Richard/Robert Gordon

Hong Kong/Mainland China: Crisp Learning Solutions, 18/F Honest Motors Building 9-11 Leighton Road, Causeway Bay, Hong Kong   Tel: 852-2915-7119, Facsimile: 852-2865-2815 ATTN: Ms. Grace Lee

Indonesia: Pt Lutan Edukasi, Citra Graha, 7th Floor, Suite 701A, Jl. Jend. Gato Subroto Kav. 35-36, Jakarta 12950 Indonesia Tel: 62-21-527-9060/527-9061 Facsimile: 62-21-527-9062 ATTN: Mr. Suwardi Luis

Japan: Phoenix Associates, Believe Mita Bldg., 8th Floor 3-43-16 Shiba, Minato-ku, Tokyo 105-0014, Japan   Tel: 81-3-5427-6231, Facsimile: 81-3-5427-6232
ATTN: Mr. Peter Owans

Malaysia, Philippines, Singapore: Epsys Pte Ltd., 540 Sims Avenue #04-01, Sims Avenue Centre, 387603, Singapore   Tel: 65-747-1964, Facsimile: 65-747-0162 ATTN: Mr. Jack Chin

CANADA

Crisp Learning Canada, 60 Briarwood Avenue, Mississauga, ON L5G 3N6 Canada
Tel: 905-274-5678, Facsimile: 905-278-2801 ATTN: Mr. Steve Connolly

EUROPEAN UNION

England: Flex Learning Media, Ltd., 9-15 Hitchin Street,
Baldock, Hertfordshire, SG7 6AL, England
Tel: 44-1-46-289-6000, Facsimile: 44-1-46-289-2417   ATTN: Mr. David Willetts

INDIA

Multi-Media HRD, Pvt. Ltd., National House, Floor 1, 6 Tulloch Road,
Appolo Bunder, Bombay, India 400-039 Tel: 91-22-204-2281,
Facsimile: 91-22-283-6478 ATTN: Messrs. Ajay Aggarwal/ C.L. Aggarwal

SOUTH AMERICA

Mexico: Grupo Editorial Iberoamerica, Nebraska 199, Col. Napoles, 03810 Mexico, D.F.
Tel: 525-523-0994, Facsimile: 525-543-1173   ATTN: Señor Nicholas Grepe

SOUTH AFRICA

Corporate: Learning Resources, PO Box 2806, Parklands, Johannesburg 2121, South Africa, Tel: 27-21-531-2923, Facsimile: 27-21-531-2944 ATTN: Mr. Ricky Robinson

MIDDLE EAST

Edutech Middle East, L.L.C., PO Box 52334, Dubai U.A.E.
Tel: 971-4-359-1222, Facsimile: 971-4-359-6500   ATTN: Mr. A.S.F. Karim